C000089170

PhotoPlus X7
Resource Guide

Contacting Serif

Help with your Product

Com👥unityPlus

community.serif.com
Get answers and ask questions in the Serif community!

Additional Serif information

Serif website   www.serif.com

Main office

Address   The Software Centre, PO Box 2000
                           Nottingham, NG11 7GW, UK

Phone   (0115) 914 2000

Phone (Registration)   (0800) 376 1989
                           +44 800 376 1989
                           800-794-6876 (US, Canada)

Phone (Sales)   (0800) 376 7070
                           +44 800 376 7070
                           800-489-6703 (US, Canada)

Customer Service   0845 345 6770
                           800-489-6720 (US, Canada)

Fax   (0115) 914 2020

Credits

This Resource Guide, and the software described in it, is furnished under an end user License Agreement, which is included with the product. The agreement specifies the permitted and prohibited uses.

Trademarks

Serif is a registered trademark of Serif (Europe) Ltd.

PhotoPlus is a registered trademark of Serif (Europe) Ltd.

All Serif product names are trademarks of Serif (Europe) Ltd.

Microsoft, Windows and the Windows logo are registered trademarks of Microsoft Corporation. All other trademarks acknowledged.

Windows Vista and the Windows Vista Start button are trademarks or registered trademarks of Microsoft Corporation in the United States and/or other countries.

Adobe Photoshop is a registered trademark of Adobe Systems Incorporated in the United States and/or other countries.

Copyrights

Digital Images © 2008 Hemera Technologies Inc. All Rights Reserved.

Portions Images ©1997-2002 Nova Development Corporation; ©1995 Expressions Computer Software; ©1996-98 CreatiCom, Inc.; ©1996-99 Cliptoart; ©1997 Multimedia Agency Corporation; ©1997-98 Seattle Support Group. Rights of all parties reserved.

The Radiance Software License, Version 1.0
Copyright © 1990 - 2002 The Regents of the University of California, through Lawrence Berkeley National Laboratory. All rights reserved.

This product includes Radiance software (http://radsite.lbl.gov/) developed by the Lawrence Berkeley National Laboratory (http://www.lbl.gov/).

Copyright © 2002-2011, Industrial Light & Magic, a division of Lucasfilm Entertainment Company Ltd. All rights reserved.

PhotoPlus Organizer was developed using LEADTOOLS, copyright ©1991-2007 LEAD Technologies, Inc. All Rights Reserved.

©2014 Serif (Europe) Ltd. All rights reserved. No part of this Resource Guide may be reproduced in any form without the express written permission of Serif (Europe) Ltd.

Serif PhotoPlus X7 © 2014 Serif (Europe) Ltd. All rights reserved.

Companies and names used in samples are fictitious.

Introduction

Welcome to the PhotoPlus X7 Resource Guide.

This Resource Guide covers the best techniques for using the fundamental tools in PhotoPlus and provides creative inspiration for your photo projects.

1: Adjusting Photos

This chapter provides exercises to help you process your raw photos and use key post-processing adjustments. It includes information on resizing, cropping, straightening, sharpening, and combining photos.

2: Creative Portraits

These project-based tutorials show you how to work with a range of PhotoPlus X7 tools, including layers and masks, to transform photos into artistic portraits. Projects include creating a black and white portrait, a colour range portrait, and a blended texture portrait.

3: Creative Showcase

Be inspired by the work in this chapter! The examples were created using brushes from the Brush Tip tab and the presets in PhotoFix and the Filter Gallery. A selection of samples provided with PhotoPlus are also shown. Instructions on accessing these areas of PhotoPlus are included.

Working with tutorials

Throughout the Resource Guide, you'll be prompted to access resource files from the **Tutorials** folder installed with PhotoPlus. These files have been provided to get you started or to help focus on a key learning point. Details for accessing these files are provided within the tutorial.

Here is a quick guide to the icons you'll find useful along the way.

 Don't forget to save your work! We'll remind you along the way with these helpful save points.

 These give you an estimate of how long a tutorial will take to complete.

 For guidance, tutorials are graded between 1 (beginner) — 5 (advanced).

 This is a note. Notes provide useful information about the program or a particular technique.

 This is a tip. Our tips provide information that will help you with your projects.

 This is a warning! We don't want to make you panic but when you see this icon, you need to pay attention to the steps as they will be particularly important.

Further Resources

- **Comprehensive PhotoPlus Help**
  The PhotoPlus Help provides information and instructions on using all the tools, features, and settings within PhotoPlus. Available via the **Help** menu (or press the **F1** key).

Exploring PhotoPlus X7

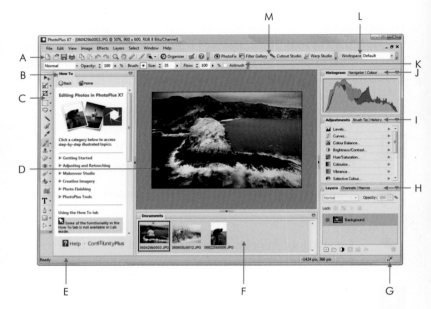

(**A**) Standard toolbar, (**B**) How To tab, (**C**) Tools toolbar, (**D**) Image "canvas", (**E**) Hintline toolbar, (**F**) Documents tab, (**G**) Snapping toggle, (**H**) Layers, Channels, and Macros tabs, (**I**) Adjustments, Brush Tip, and History tabs, (**J**) Histogram, Navigator, and Colour tabs, (**K**) Context toolbar, (**L**) Workspace toolbar, (**M**) Photo Studio toolbar.

The PhotoPlus workspace

The PhotoPlus studio workspace consists of:

- Your photo canvas.

- The **Documents** tab, which displays all of your open photos.

- The **How To** tab, where many commands can be applied automatically.

- A range of photo-specific **tabs**, to help you organize your workflow and make photo adjustments.

- Horizontal and vertical **toolbars**, used to access PhotoPlus commands and tools.

Move the mouse pointer around the screen and you'll see popup **tooltips** that identify toolbar buttons and flyouts.

Right-click any object or page region to bring up a **context menu** of functions.

Table of Contents

Adjusting Photos

1

Raw images

20 min

When you take a photo as a raw file, you are essentially saving an unprocessed photo. It's a 'digital negative' and needs to be developed. PhotoPlus has a digital dark room called Import Raw for just this purpose.

In this tutorial, we'll look at some basic corrections and settings that you can apply to your raw file in the Import Raw dialog.

CR2

Unfortunately, as raw files are so large, we can't provide a file for you to use, but the steps in the tutorial will work with any photo with similar exposure problems. Remember, there are no hard and fast rules. Corrections are mainly done by eye and are specific to each individual photo.

By the end of this tutorial you will be able to:

- Open a raw photo file.

- Crop a photo.

- Adjust white balance and change exposure.

- Reduce noise.

Let's begin...

Our example photos were simultaneously taken as a JPEG and raw file.

The photo above shows how heavily underexposed the JPEG was. Luckily, we can use the raw file to allow us to make adjustments to dramatically improve the exposure.

To open a raw photo, choose one of the following:

- On the **Standard** toolbar, click  **Open**. In the **Open** dialog, navigate to and select your raw file, and then click **Open**.

- Drag and drop a raw file from Windows Explorer onto the empty workspace.

The photo opens in the **Import Raw** dialog.

The Import Raw dialog automatically applies some correction to your image and this might be all that's needed. However, the dialog comes with a variety of tools which allow you to adjust your image further. We'll apply a white balance correction, reduce the noise, and modify the exposure. But first, we'll crop our image.

Cropping

The main reason for cropping a photo is to improve its overall composition. However, if you crop before doing any other corrective procedures, it will help you better evaluate the adjustments needed. Cropping unwanted areas will mean you can focus adjustments on the desirable area only, therefore getting the best from the settings you apply. Let's take a look at this now.

To crop a photo:

1. On the **Retouch Tools** toolbar, click the ⌗ **Crop and Straighten tool**.

2. On the **Crop** section, select 🔒 lock to ensure the **Aspect Ratio** remains as **Original**.

3. In the preview window, drag the corner handles of the crop area to position the crop (using the thirds grid as a guide).

4. When you're happy with the crop, click ✅ **Accept**.

Not only can you see the difference in the composition, you will also notice the difference in the photo's histogram.

White balance

Our photo has a red cast. We can see this in the photo itself and by looking at the histogram.

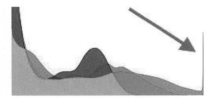

To correct the white balance:

1.  From the **Filters: Global**, on the **White Balance** filter, click the **Set white level**.

2. Click on a light area of your photo that should be a neutral reference point.

3. You can also adjust the **Temp**, **Tint**, and **Saturation** settings to fine-tune the image's white balance.

The white balance is updated. If it's not quite right, click on another area until a natural colour balance is achieved.

Notice that the histogram is also updated to show the change in tonal balance.

Changing exposure

If the photo is still too dark, we can use the sliders to increase the exposure. It's important to be careful not to do this too much otherwise you risk losing detail in the lighter areas of the photo.

To increase the photo exposure:

1. From the **Filters: Global**, on the **Lighting** filter, increase the **Exposure** by dragging the slider.

Aim for small increments and let the preview pane update each time before you make further adjustments. In our example, an Exposure adjustment of 0.3 is enough just to lift the photo.

Notice that the histogram has spread out again while retaining the shape it had after the white balance adjustment.

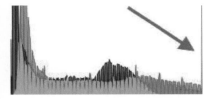

Ideally, keep an eye on the histogram and make sure that you stop before clipping occurs at the right edge. Sometimes, as in our example, clipping is unavoidable if you want to bring out the detail in the darker areas.

Curves

Our example image is still a little dark. We'll apply this adjustment now using Curves.

To lighten an image using Curves:

1. From the **Filters: Global**, click ☐ **Enable** to activate the **Curves** filter and then click ▷ **Expand/Collapse filter** to display the adjustment settings (i.e. the Curves graph).

2.   Drag the graph upwards.

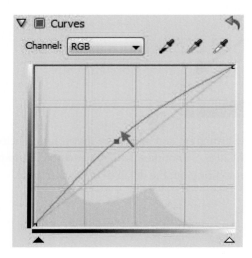

A gentle upward (convex) curve lightens the shadows and increases contrast.

Our photo already suffered from noise and our previous adjustments have further accentuated this. This can be fixed with the noise reduction adjustment.

Noise reduction

Photos taken using a high ISO setting, or those that are underexposed like our example, often suffer with "digital noise". Noise is normally displayed as pixels of an unexpected, often brighter colour.

We can reduce the noise in a photo by using the noise reduction filter.

To reduce noise:

1. From the **Filters: Global**, click ▢ **Enable** to activate the **Noise Reduction** filter.

    The **Noise Reduction** filter will be applied at the default settings.

2. To adjust the settings, click ▷ **Expand/Collapse filter** and then:

    *   Increase the **Colour** slider to eradicate randomly placed colour pixels which constitute the most noticeable areas of noise.

    *   Increase the **Luminance** slider to reduce areas where pixels are unnaturally lighter or darker than surrounding pixels.

The adjustments to this photo in the Import Raw dialog are complete!

Importing into main workspace

With all your raw adjustments made, it's now time to complete the import of your file and open it in PhotoPlus's main workspace for saving, exporting or further adjusting.

To complete raw import:

* In the **Import Raw** dialog, set the **Output Format** using the **Bit Depth** and **Colour** drop-down lists, and then click **OK**.

  Your processed raw file opens in the workspace.

We left the format set to 16 Bits/Channel so we could continue to edit our photo at the highest quality possible.

If you wish to apply further adjustments to your photo, check out **Key Adjustments** on p. 33. For more information on the settings available in the Import Raw dialog, see **Adjusting raw images** in PhotoPlus Help.

 Exporting your completed image to a common image file format will allow you to get full use from it. See the **Saving and exporting** tutorial on p. 75 for more information.

Resizing and resampling

10 min

There may be times when you want to use a photo but it's too big or too small for the purpose. The best way to solve this problem is to resize (or resample) the photo. We'll show you how in this tutorial.

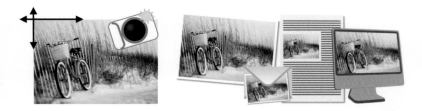

By the end of this tutorial you will be able to:

- Resize (scale) a photo for print.

- Resample a photo for print.

- Resample a photo for screen viewing.

- Optimize file sizes for websites and sharing.

Let's begin...

1. On the **Standard** toolbar, click  **Open**.

2. In the **Open** dialog, navigate to and select your photo, and then click **Open**.

    The photo opens in the workspace.

Our photo was taken using a digital camera and measures 4272 x 2848 pixels.

Resizing vs Resampling

A typical monitor resolution is either 72 pixels per inch (ppi) or 96 ppi. This is what controls a photo's size on screen. When you print a photo, the pixels are printed as small dots. The number of dots per inch gives a photo its dpi setting. A high quality photo print will be printed at 300 dots per inch (dpi).

There are two ways to change the size of a photo—resizing and resampling. What's the difference? Although often used interchangeably, there's actually an important difference between the two.

- **Resizing**, otherwise known as scaling, changes the size at which the photo will print, without changing the number of pixels in the photo. Resizing determines whether the pixels are printed further apart (to print it bigger) or closer together (to print it smaller). Resizing a photo will not affect screen display.

- **Resampling** changes the number of pixels in the photo. This is the only way that you can change the size at which a photo will display on screen. When resampling, dpi settings are ignored.

  For printing small photos at an increased size, you may need to resample them first while maintaining a certain dpi print resolution.

Both methods are available in PhotoPlus via the Image Size dialog.

Resizing photos for print

The only time that you'll really resize (scale) a photo is when you want to print it. Remember, resizing does not modify the photo in any way. Obviously, to get a good print you'll need to maintain a certain dpi—200dpi will produce an excellent home print; aim for 300dpi for a professional print.

To resize (scale) a photo:

1.   From the **Image** menu, click **Image Size**.

2.   In the **Image Size** dialog:

•   Uncheck **Resize layers**.

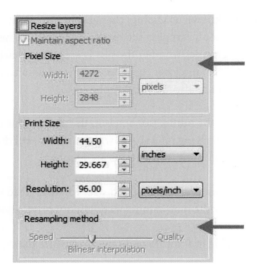

All resampling options are greyed out.

In the Print Size section, the current Width, Height and Resolution dimensions are displayed.

The native resolution of our photo is 96 dpi. At this resolution, as the dialog shows us, the photo will print at approximately 44.5 x 29.7 inches!

- To force the photo to print at 300dpi, in the **Resolution** box, type '300' and press the **Tab** key.

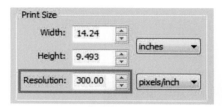

The printing Width and Height update automatically to approximately 14.2 x 9.5 inches.

- Alternatively, to specify exact print dimensions, in the **Width** box, type the width you want the photo to print at (e.g. 21.00) and press the **Tab** key.

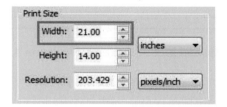

The Height and Resolution values will update to match.

- When you are happy with the print size, click **OK.**

At first it might seem like nothing has changed. This is somewhat true! Your photo remains unaltered and your monitor still displays it at its native resolution. However, the change is apparent when you come to print it.

The following illustration shows how our photo will print with the two settings we mentioned on the previous page.

14.2 x 9.5 inches at 300 dpi and 21 x 14 inches at 200 dpi on A3 landscape paper

The photo's dimensions have been compressed or expanded to change the size of the printed photo, but the photo itself remains unchanged.

If you use the 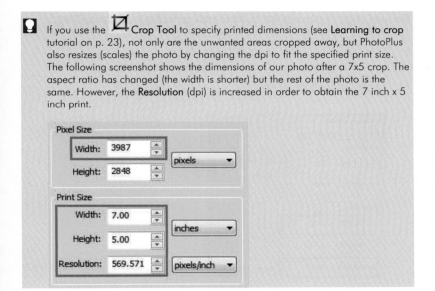Crop Tool to specify printed dimensions (see **Learning to crop** tutorial on p. 23), not only are the unwanted areas cropped away, but PhotoPlus also resizes (scales) the photo by changing the dpi to fit the specified print size. The following screenshot shows the dimensions of our photo after a 7x5 crop. The aspect ratio has changed (the width is shorter) but the rest of the photo is the same. However, the **Resolution** (dpi) is increased in order to obtain the 7 inch x 5 inch print.

Pixel Size
Width: 3987 pixels
Height: 2848

Print Size
Width: 7.00 inches
Height: 5.00
Resolution: 569.571 pixels/inch

Resampling photos for print, screen, and the web

There are many times when you want to create a larger or smaller version of your photo—to create a large, high quality print, to create a small file to share via email, or to create a lower resolution photo for your website. In each case, you'll need to change the number of pixels in the actual photo, i.e. **resample** it. We'll show you how to do this without the distortion that resampling can sometimes introduce.

We'll start by creating a 300dpi A3 landscape poster print of our photo. To ensure that the print goes right to the edges, we'll increase our photo print size to approximately 23 inches x 15 inches.

To enlarge a photo to a 300 dpi print by resampling:

1. From the **Image** menu, click **Image Size**.

2. In the **Image Size** dialog:

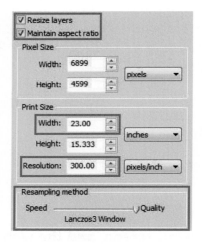

- Ensure the **Resize layers** option is selected.

- Ensure the **Maintain aspect ratio** option is selected.

- In the **Print Size** section set the **Resolution** to **300**.

- If necessary, set the required print **Width** or **Height**.

  If **Maintain aspect ratio** is selected (recommended), when you change the width, the height updates correspondingly and vice versa.

As you can see, in our example the overall pixel size of the photo is automatically increased from 4272 x 2848 to 6899 x 4599.

- Drag the **Resampling method** slider to **Lanczos 3 Window** (this is the 'best' but slowest resampling method)

- Click **OK**.

PhotoPlus resamples the photo to the new size ready for printing.

After resampling a photo, you may need to sharpen the details. Try using the Unsharp Mask on the Effects > Sharpen menu to sharpen your photo before printing. For more on using the Unsharp Mask, see the Sharpening blurred photos tutorial on p. 53.

Make sure you save your resampled photo as a new file and be sure not to overwrite the original!

Save now! Click **File > Save As** and choose a new name for your file.

To change photo dimensions for screen, email and the web:

1. From the **Image** menu, click **Image Size**.

2. In the **Image Size** dialog:

   - Ensure the **Resize layers** option is selected.

   - Ensure the **Maintain aspect ratio** option is selected.

- In the **Pixel Size** section set the required screen **Width** or **Height**—setting the largest dimension to around 800 pixels works well.

  If **Maintain aspect ratio** is selected (recommended), when you change the width, the height will automatically update and vice versa.

- Drag the **Resampling method** slider to **Lanczos 3 Window** (this is the 'best' but slowest resampling method)

- Click **OK**.

 Remember, only pixel dimensions are important when resizing a photo for screen viewing purposes as all dpi settings are ignored.

 Save now! Click **File** > **Save As** and choose a new name for your file.

Resizing photos when exporting

If you want to resize a photo for a specific reason, e.g. to add it to a website, you might find it easier to use the **Export Optimizer** dialog. On export, an entirely new copy of the photo is created, resampled to the dimensions you specify. This means you don't need to permanently resample your original photo.

We look at this process in full in **Saving and exporting** on p. 75.

Learning to crop

15 min

Every photo has boundaries, and you can decide where those boundaries should be. Cropping is an easy, yet often overlooked, step when editing photos. In this tutorial, we'll show you how to use the various tools in PhotoPlus to crop your photos to add visual impact and focus.

By the end of this tutorial you will be able to:

•   Define a crop selection size using the Crop Tool.

•   Use the Thirds Grid to aid photo composition.

•   Crop to a pre-defined print size.

•   Convert a photo from landscape to portrait.

Let's begin...

1. On the **Standard** toolbar, click  **Open**.

2. In the **Open** dialog, navigate to the **Tutorials** folder.

> In a standard installation, the image files can be accessed from the following location:
>
> C:\Program Files\Serif\PhotoPlus\X7\Tutorials or
> C:\Program Files (x86)\Serif\PhotoPlus\X7\Tutorials
>
> However, the path may differ if you changed the installation location.

3. Select **11.jpg** and click **Open**.

The photo opens in the workspace.

Cropping a photo

By default, when you crop a photo, PhotoPlus hides all of the pixels outside the crop selection area. The canvas size is automatically resized to show only the area inside the crop selection.

 You can crop larger areas when photos are shot at a high resolution. Keep this in mind before taking photos and make sure your camera is set to its highest resolution and photo quality.

To crop a photo with Crop Tool:

1. On the **Tools** toolbar, select the **Crop Tool**.

2. Drag out a rectangular crop selection area on the photo. (To constrain the region to a square, hold down the **Ctrl** key while dragging.)

    The area that will be hidden turns dark.

3. If required, click and drag inside the selection to move the whole crop area (the cursor changes to the **Move** cursor), or drag the sizing handles to resize.

4. On the context toolbar, click  **Apply crop**.

Save now! Click **File > Save As** and choose a new name for your file.

> If you intend on making any further adjustments to your photo, it's worth saving the file as an .spp file. This will also allow you to increase the cropped area at a later date, if necessary.

Using the Rule of Thirds

The Crop Tool comes with a handy component which helps you compose your photo by cropping while using the Rule of Thirds.

To use the Rule of Thirds grid:

1.   On the **Tools** toolbar, select the 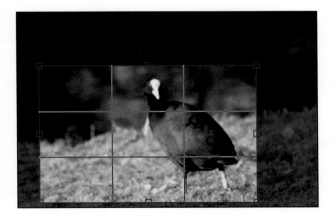 **Crop Tool**.

2.   On the context toolbar, select the **Thirds grid** option.

3.   Drag to define your crop area—a 3 x 3 grid is superimposed within your crop selection area.

For best results, position the subject of the photo at any of the four intersection points on the grid.

4. On the context toolbar, click  **Apply crop**.

As you can see, a close crop can enhance or change the focus of a photo.

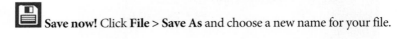 **Save now!** Click **File > Save As** and choose a new name for your file.

Cropping to a standard print size

Some digital photographs sizes do not comply with the standard print sizes—i.e. 6x4, 7x5, 8x10—but the Crop Tool comes with presets to help you crop specifically to these sizes.

To crop to a pre-defined print size:

1. On the **Tools** toolbar, select the **Crop Tool**.

2. On the context toolbar, from the left-most drop-down list, select **10 x 8 in**.

3. Drag out to define your crop selection area.

4. On the context toolbar, click ✅ **Apply crop**.

The print resolution adjusts to honour the print dimensions. You can now export your photo and upload it to an online printing service or take it to a kiosk or photo processing shop for printing (see **Saving and exporting** on p. 75) or print at home directly from PhotoPlus (see **Printing** in PhotoPlus Help)!

 Save now! Click **File > Save As** and choose a new name for your file.

Change the orientation of a photo

You can also use the pre-defined print sizes to change the orientation of a photo.

To change a photo from landscape to portrait:

1. On the **Tools** toolbar, select the  **Crop Tool**.

2. On the context toolbar, from the left-most drop-down list, select **4 x 6 in**.

3. Drag out to define your crop selection area.

4.   On the context toolbar, click **Apply crop**.

The applied crop converts your landscape orientation to portrait orientation.

 You can, of course, convert a photo from portrait to landscape too!

We applied a 6 x 4 in crop to our portrait photo to convert it to landscape.

That's it! You now know the many ways you can use the Crop Tool to adjust and enhance your photos.

 Save now! Click **File** > **Save As** and choose a new name for your file.

Key Adjustments

 15 min

This tutorial takes you through the various methods you can use to enhance and improve a photograph.

By the end of this tutorial you will be able to:

- Straighten the horizon in a photo.

- Apply a Vibrance adjustment to enhance colours.

- Make Levels and Curves adjustments.

Straightening horizons in photos

It's not always easy to get the horizon straight when taking photos, particularly when you're more focused on getting other elements right. However, sometimes even the slightest offset can confuse the eye and ruin a perfectly good photo. The Straighten Tool allows you to straighten the horizon instantly.

> ⚠ Straightening a photo is a permanent process—depending on the settings, some of the photo may be discarded! The best approach is to save a copy of your photo first and apply the straighten to the copy.

> 💡 PhotoPlus can also intelligently straightens photos vertically. Simply follow the procedure below, drawing a line along a vertical edge.

To straighten a photo:

1. Follow the procedure on p. 24 to open **22.jpg**.

2. On the **Tools** toolbar, from the **Crop Tools** flyout, select the **Straighten Tool**.

3. On the context toolbar:

    •   From the **Canvas** drop-down list, ensure **Crop** is selected.

    •   (Optional) If you're working on a multi-layer photo and wish to straighten only the selected layer, deselect **Rotate All Layers**.

4. Drag a line across your photo to define your new horizon.

Your photo will automatically realign according to the line you have defined and will be cropped to remove any empty areas resulting from the straighten adjustment.

A photo can sometimes be enhanced by cropping (covered in more details in **Learning to crop** on p. 23).

 Save now! Click **File > Save As** and choose a new name for your file.

Enhancing colour using Vibrance

The Vibrance adjustment subtly enriches the colours in your photo without saturating skin tones. This can give your photo an authentic but bold finish. Even the slightest increase can have a dramatic impact.

To apply a vibrance adjustment:

1. Follow the procedure on p. 24 to open **33.jpg**.

2. On the **Adjustments** tab:

    -   Click **Vibrance**. The tab updates to display the settings for the selected adjustment.

    -   Drag the **Vibrance** slider to the right to saturate colours.

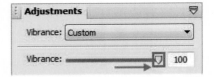

We set our value to **100**.

In our worked example, the colours are now much richer. Skin tones have been warmed lightly, but still retain a natural tone.

Adjusting Levels

The Levels adjustment displays a histogram showing the proportion of
photo pixels at each lightness value, ranging from shadows through to
highlights. By looking at the histogram, you can see if the photo lacks a
'high end' or a 'low end' or is 'washed out', and adjust the **black** or **white**
point(s) accordingly.

To apply a preset Levels adjustment:

1.   Follow the procedure on p. 24 to open **44.jpg**.

2.   On the **Adjustments** tab:

   •   Click **Levels**.

        The tab updates to display the settings for the selected
        adjustment.

        The histogram on the **Adjustments** tab, shows that the photo is
        lacking a low end and the highlights are also clipped (indicated
        by the sharp peak on the right).

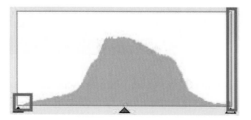

- From the **Levels** drop-down list, select **Increase Contrast**.

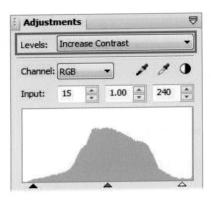

Notice the black and white points have automatically moved inwards.

Our photo instantly loses its 'washed out' appearance.

This may be all the photo needs, however, we can increase the contrast further by adjusting the photo's levels more.

Save now! Click **File** > **Save As** and choose a new name for your file.

To customize a Levels adjustment:

- On the **Adjustments** tab:

    - Drag the black point slider further to the right to an **Input** level around **50**.

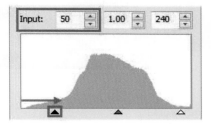

    - Drag the white point slider further to the left to an **Input** level around **220**.

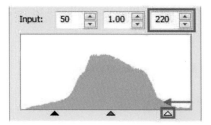

The contrast in the photo increases further and the colours are enhanced.

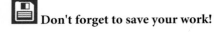 **Don't forget to save your work!**

So far, we have been setting the overall levels for the photo on the Red, Green, and Blue channels combined. For more control, you can modify the Red, Green and Blue channels individually. This allows you to add emphasis to one channel over others. This can result in a richer, more refined finish.

To apply an advanced Levels adjustment:

- On the **Adjustments** tab:

- Click ↩ **Restore default settings**.

   This resets the Levels adjustment back to that of the original photo.

- From the **Channel** drop-down list, select **Blue**.

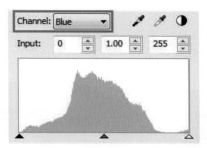

The histogram updates to show the Blue channel only.

The histogram is not dramatically different to the RGB histogram, but the highlights are lacking.

- Drag the white point to the left to an **Input** level around **205**.

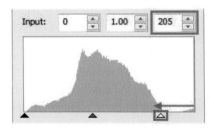

This adjustment adds more definition to the highlights in the Blue channel, but also gives the photo a cold, blue cast. We can remove this colour cast by adjusting the levels further.

- Drag the black point to the right to an **Input** level around **30**.

- Finally, select and adjust the **Green** and **Red** channels as needed until you are happy with the results.

  We set our Green channel to **Input 39, 226** and our Red channel to **Input 25, 225**.

 Save now! Click **File** > **Save As** and choose a new name for your file.

Adjusting Curves

Probably the professional photographer's favourite adjustment. The Curves adjustment lets you correct the tonal range of a photo—the spread of lightness values through shadow, midtone, and highlight regions—and control individual colour components. It gives the greatest control of the midtones and, when used carefully, really enhances a photo.

The adjustments you're likely to make include:

- Dragging the curves line down to darken photo midtones.

- Dragging the curves line up to lighten the midtones.

- Creating a gentle S-shape to correct washed out photos.

To apply a preset Curves adjustment:

1. Follow the procedure on p. 24 to open **44.jpg**.

   We'll use a Curves adjustment to enhance the photo's contrast by deepening shadows and lightening highlights.

2. On the **Adjustments** tab:

   • Click **Curves**.

   The tab updates to display the settings for the selected adjustment.

   • From the **Curves** drop-down list, select **Contrast**.

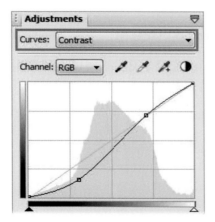

   The gentle S-shape deepens the shadows, lightens the highlights, and increases contrast.

Our photo instantly loses its 'washed out' appearance.

This may be all the photo needs, however, we're going to tweak our Curves adjustment to increase the highlights further.

 Save now! Click **File > Save As** and choose a new name for your file.

To customize a Curves adjustment:

- On the **Adjustments** tab, drag the right point upwards until the **Output** is around **204**.

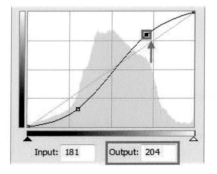

The increased intensity in the photo's highlights is exactly what we're seeking.

This is probably the most difficult adjustment to master, but with practice, it produces some great results! Your photos will display a greater level of contrast, sharpened details, and boosted colours.

You can also make Curves adjustments to individual Red, Green, and Blue channels for additional control. See the **To apply an advanced Levels adjustment** section on p. 40 for more information.

Finding the Curves adjustment complex and fiddly? You can also use a variety of blend modes to correct the exposure problems, see **Correcting exposure** on the following page for quick and easy fixes!

That's it! We've quickly run through some key adjustments you can apply to your photos. A comprehensive list of the adjustments available in PhotoPlus, and instructions on working with them, are available in PhotoPlus Help.

Don't forget to save your work! Also see the **Saving and exporting** tutorial on p. 75 for more information.

Correcting exposure

 15 min

Whatever your experience as a photographer, chances are you'll have some photos which are either overexposed (too bright), underexposed (too dark) or 'washed out'. Don't despair! We'll show you how to fix common exposure problems quickly without going anywhere near a complicated Curves adjustment!

For information on correcting exposure problems in raw photos, see **Raw images** on p. 3.

By the end of this tutorial you will be able to:

* Duplicate a layer.

* Apply a Multiply blend mode to correct overexposure.

* Apply a Screen blend mode to correct underexposure.

* Enhance washed out photos using an Overlay blend mode.

Let's begin...

- Follow the procedure on p. 24 to open **55.jpg**.

  To quickly fix our exposure problems, we will need two identical layers to blend together...

Duplicating a layer

PhotoPlus makes it easy to duplicate a layer from the Layers tab.

To create a duplicate layer:

1. On the **Layers** tab, right-click the **Background** layer, and select **Duplicate**.

2. In the **Duplicate Layer** dialog, accept the default settings and click **OK**.

    A duplicate layer, called **Background Copy**, is added to the Layers tab.

Now we'll apply a blend mode to correct an overexposed photo.

Correcting overexposure

Overexposure describes a photo which is too bright, and has therefore lost detail, due to being exposed to too much light. Multiply is the best blend mode to use to rescue overexposed photos! It has the effect of decreasing exposure in the darker areas, while keeping the lighter areas relatively unchanged.

To apply a blend mode:

- On the **Layers** tab:

- Click to select **Background Copy**.

- From the blend mode drop-down list, select **Multiply**.

 If the effect is too strong, you can always reduce the layer's Opacity on the Layers tab.

Next we'll apply a blend mode to correct an underexposed photo.

 Save now! Click **File** > **Save As** and choose a new name for your file.

When saving, you may receive a warning message recommending you save your file as a PhotoPlus picture. Click OK to save as an .spp file so you can modify changes at a later date if necessary.

Correcting underexposure

Underexposure describes a photo which is too dark, and has therefore lost detail, because of a lack of exposure to light. The Screen blend mode can be used to increase brightness in a photo, while retaining tonal balance. This has the effect of increasing exposure in the darkest areas, while keeping the lighter areas relatively unchanged.

To apply a blend mode:

1.   Follow the procedure on p. 24 to open **66.jpg**.

2.   Repeat the procedure to duplicate the **Background** layer (see p. 48).

3.   On the **Layers** tab:

- Click to select **Background Copy**.

- From the blend mode drop-down list, select **Screen**.

   The photo's overall lightness instantly increases but is slightly too much.

- Set the **Opacity** to **85%**.

It's best to use multiple duplicate layers and apply the multiply effect in increments. Don't be afraid to use several layers, each set to only 10% or 15% Opacity as this is likely to produce a more balanced result.

Next we'll look into correcting a 'washed out' photo.

Save now! Click **File** > **Save As** and choose a new name for your file.

Enhancing a washed out photo

Washed out photos tend to have a grey tone caused by a lack of contrast between light and dark areas. The Overlay and Soft Light blend modes act by lightening highlights and deepening shadows to produce a well contrasted photo. They both also make colours in a photo more vibrant and reduce haze from landscape photos.

To apply a blend mode:

1. Follow the procedure on p. 24 to open **44.jpg**.

2. Repeat the procedure to duplicate the **Background** layer (see p. 48).

3. On the **Layers** tab:

- Click to select **Background Copy**.

- From the blend mode drop-down list, select **Overlay**.

  The photo's contrast instantly improves, but is overpowering.

- Set the **Opacity** to **75%**.

If you find the **Overlay** blend mode is too strong, try selecting **Soft Light** instead.

If you're looking for more refined control when adjusting the exposure of your photos, why not try a Curves adjustment? For more information, see **Key Adjustments: Adjusting Curves** on p. 42.

Don't forget to save your work! Also see the **Saving and exporting** tutorial on p. 75 for more information.

Sharpening blurred photos

 15 min

We've all found ourselves in the frustrating situation of discovering that a photo, which looked perfect on our digital camera's LCD screen, is blurry when we view it on the computer. Rather than throw the photo away, you can use PhotoPlus to add clarity or sharpen the photo.

We'll show you several sharpening techniques which you can experiment with.

By the end of this tutorial you will be able to:

•   Create a duplicate layer and convert it to a filter layer.

•   Apply a quick Clarity adjustment.

•   Sharpen using High Pass filter with an Overlay blend mode.

•   Use an Unsharp Mask filter.

Let's begin...

- Follow the procedure on p. 24 to open **11.jpg**.

The photo opens in the workspace.

Now we can explore a few techniques to help sharpen this photo—
beginning with a quick adjustment and then moving on to more
professional techniques.

 Some of the adjustments made in this exercise can be applied directly to a photo,
but for best practice we'll be using **adjustment layers** and **filter layers**.

Adjustment layers and filter layers provide more flexibility and let you apply
changes experimentally without affecting your original photo. You can turn these
layers on and off to compare 'before' and 'after' states, and can easily edit and
delete them later.

Duplicating a layer and converting to a filter layer

PhotoPlus makes it easy to duplicate a layer from the **Layers** tab and then convert it to a filter layer.

To create a duplicate layer:

1. On the **Layers** tab, right-click the **Background** layer, and select **Duplicate**.

2. In the **Duplicate Layer** dialog, in the **As** input box type 'Clarity' and click **OK**.

   A duplicate layer, called Clarity, is added to the Layers tab.

Now to convert it to a filter layer for maximum flexibility...

To convert a standard layer to a filter layer:

- On the **Layers** tab, right-click on the new **Clarity** layer and click **Convert to Filter Layer**.

Now to look at clarity and sharpening.

Technique 1: Adjusting Clarity

The Clarity adjustment uses a contrast filter to quickly remove minor blur and softness from a photo—it may be all you need to improve your photo. Let's see what impact it has on our example photo...

To apply a clarity adjustment:

1. On the **Layers** tab, select the **Clarity** layer.

2. From the **Image** menu, click **Adjust > Clarity**.

3. In the **Clarity** dialog:

   - Drag the slider to the right to increase the **Clarity** to **80.0**.

   - Click **OK**.

The Clarity adjustment has added more definition to the feathers and grass.

 Save now! Click **File > Save As** and choose a new name for your file.

When saving, you may receive a warning message recommending you save your file as a PhotoPlus picture. Click OK to save as an .spp file so you can modify changes at a later date if necessary.

Technique 2: Sharpening using High Pass

At first the **High Pass** filter may only appear to be useful for creative, artistic effects. However, when combined with a layer blend mode, it's a highly customizable and effective way of sharpening blurred photos.

To add a High Pass filter:

1. On the **Layers** tab:

    -   Click **Hide/Show Layer** next to the **Clarity** layer to hide it.

    -   Repeat the procedure to duplicate the **Background** layer and convert it to a filter layer (see p. 55), this time naming the layer **High Pass**.

    -   Select the **High Pass** layer.

2. From the **Effects** menu, click **Other > High Pass**.

3. In the **High Pass** dialog:

    -   Drag the slider to the right to increase the **Radius** to **5.0**.

    -   Click **OK**.

4. The High Pass effect is applied to the layer.

5. On the **Layers** tab, from the blend mode drop-down list, select **Overlay**.

The High Pass effect adds definition to all the lines in the foreground, giving the photo an overall sharper appearance.

 Try experimenting by setting the blend mode to **Soft Light** or **Hard Light** to soften or strengthen the sharpening effect, respectively.

Don't forget to save your work!

Technique 3: Applying an Unsharp Mask

Unsharp Mask works mainly to enhance the edges in a photo. It's excellent for improving photo quality, especially with scanned or resized pictures.

To apply an Unsharp Mask:

1. On the **Layers** tab:

   • Click ◳ **Hide/Show Layer** next to the **High Pass** layer to hide it.

- Repeat the procedure to duplicate the **Background** layer and convert it to a filter layer (see p. 55), this time naming the layer **Unsharp Mask**.

- Select the **Unsharp Mask** layer.

2. From the **Effects** menu, click **Sharpen > Unsharp Mask**.

3. In the **Unsharp Mask** dialog:

Amount:	60	%
Radius:	85.0	pixels
Threshold:	0	levels

- Set the **Amount** to **60**.

- Set the **Radius** to **85.0**.

In general, use a higher **Radius** setting for higher resolution photos intended for print, and a lower radius for lower resolution photos that will be viewed on screen.

- Set the **Threshold** to **0**.

Set the threshold too high and you'll see very little change in your photo. Generally, values between 0 and 5 are useful. Use a higher threshold for grainy photos or skin tones (5 or sometimes more), so the filter won't merely amplify noise in the photo.

- Click **OK**.

Note especially the increase in depth and colour.

 Don't forget to save your work! Also see the **Saving and exporting** tutorial on p. 75 for more information.

That's it! The techniques we've explored in this tutorial all give slightly different sharpening results. You can choose the method you prefer, or the one which works best for your specific photo.

 You can switch between the effects using ▣ Hide/Show Layer on the Layers tab.

Moreover, you can also experiment with combining any of these techniques! The photo below uses the Unsharp Mask set as above with the High Pass effect set to a Soft Light blend mode and 50% Opacity.

Combining photos

15 min

One advantage of digital cameras is the ability to take (almost) limitless photos—in fact, you may find you frequently take several shots in quick succession to try and get the best from a scene. What happens if you have almost identical scenes but like different sections from each? You can use PhotoPlus to combine them.

By the end of this tutorial you will be able to:

- Add and align photos in a single project.

- Combine photos using a mask.

- Prepare for future compositional shots.

Let's begin...

1.   Follow the procedure on p. 24 to open **A.jpg**.

2.   Repeat to open **B.jpg**.

The second photo opens in the workspace and both are displayed in the Documents tab.

We are going to examine how to use a mask to combine these to create a composition where our female model is looking at the camera and our male model is looking to the side.

Aligning multiple photos in a single project

Before we get to the masking, we first need to place our photos in the same project.

To copy and paste as new layer:

1.   On the **Documents** tab, click to select **B.jpg**.

2.   From the **Edit** menu, click **Copy** (or press **Ctrl+C**).

3.   On the **Documents** tab, click to select **A.jpg**.

4.   From the **Edit** menu, click **Paste>As New Layer** (or press **Ctrl+L**).

The copied photo is displayed in the workspace and added to the Layers tab as **Layer 1**.

With both photos now in the same project, the next step is to align them.

To align two photos:

1.   On the **Layers** tab, select **Layer 1** and reduce the **Opacity** to **60%**.

2.   On the **Tools** toolbar, select the  **Deform Tool**.

3. Examine the photos for suitable reference points—we chose the edges of the bench to the left and right of our models.

4. Drag and rotate the photo on **Layer 1** until the reference points match up.

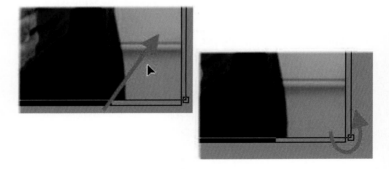

5. When you're happy with the alignment, on the **Layers** tab, increase the **Opacity** of **Layer 1** to **100%**.

If you're completing this tutorial using your own photos and there is a disparity between the size of objects within your photos, you can also use the **Deform Tool** to increase or decrease the photo on **Layer 1** to match the **Background** layer. Remember to hold down the **Shift** key as you resize your photo to constrain its aspect ratio.

With the photos now correctly aligned, we can begin revealing the Background layer through Layer 1.

 Save now! Click **File** > **Save As** and choose a new name for your file.

 When saving, you may receive a warning message recommending you save your file as a PhotoPlus picture. Click **OK** to save as an .spp file so you can modify changes at a later date if necessary.

Masking

Masking is the process of hiding pixels on one layer to reveal the layer underneath. Masks can be added to layers as 'reveal all' (the layer it is applied to is fully visible), 'hide all' (the layer it is applied to is rendered invisible), or a combination of both. If a selection is in place when the mask is applied, the pixels within the selection are set to 'reveal all' while those outside of the selection are set to 'hide all'.

We'll create our mask by starting with a selection.

To create a selection:

1. From the **Tools** toolbar, from the **Shape Selection Tools** flyout, select **Rectangle Selection Tool**.

2. From the top, right of the photo, drag down and to the left to draw a rectangle which encompasses our male model.

3. Release the mouse button to create the selection.

With the selection in place, let's create our mask!

To create a mask:

* On the **Layers** tab, select **Layer 1** and then click  **Add Layer Mask**.

  A mask is added to Layer 1 and selected by default.

On the Layers tab, you will notice that half of the mask is black, while the other half is white. Black represents 'hide all' on a mask, while white represents 'reveal all'. The selection has done a good job in hiding part of the layer, while revealing another, but it's not perfect. Let's now remove the selection and look at how we can modify the mask.

To remove a selection:

1. From the **Select** menu, click **Deselect** (or press **Ctrl+D**).

2. On the **Standard** toolbar, select the  **Zoom Tool** and drag on the photo to zoom into the area between the two models.

You can clearly see the boundaries between the two photos. We'll modify the mask to smoothly combine the photos.

To edit a mask:

1. On the **Tools** toolbar, select the 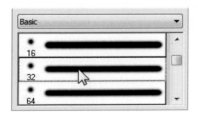 **Paintbrush Tool**.

2. On the **Brush Tip** tab, select **Basic** from the drop-down list, and then select the **32 pixel** soft brush.

3.   On the **Colour** tab, ensure the foreground colour is set to **black**.

4.   Begin painting along the seam to hide the top photo and reveal the background photo.

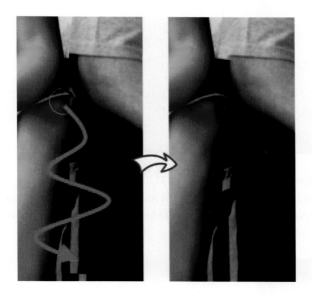

You will notice the mask thumbnail on Layer 1 (Layers tab) update as you paint.

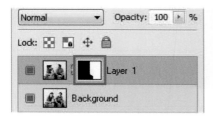

5. The sports trousers are blended with ease but the male model's shirt may cause some overlap issues.

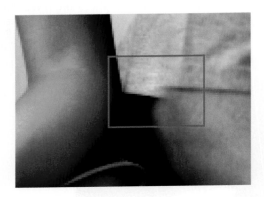

6. If you encounter the same problem as illustrated above, on the **Colour** tab, ensure the foreground colour is set to **white** and paint over the problem area. This hides the background photo and reveals the top photo again.

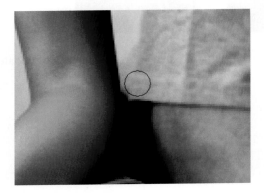

You may find reducing the size and opacity of the brush will give the precision and accuracy needed for this detailed work.

7.   Continue painting, switching between black and white, until you are happy with the results.

The alignment and rotation of the top layer has resulted in an unavoidable poor edge at the bottom right of the photo. This, however, can be instantly rectified with a crop. (We applied a preset **7 x 5 in** crop.)

That's it! This resulting, combined photo looks excellent. Feel free to explore these techniques on your own photos.

Don't forget to save your work! Also see the **Saving and exporting** tutorial on p. 75 for more information.

💡 **Group photo tips**

When taking group photos, you'll invariably end up with some people looking at the camera while others are looking away, and some people smiling while others are talking. Using these techniques, you'll be able to compose the perfect group portraits.

If you have the luxury of planning a composite shot, the following tips should help you compile the final photo quicker:

- Use a tripod to position the camera and do not adjust it between shots—this will remove the need to align the photos.

- Set the zoom and do not adjust it between shots—this will remove the need to resize the photos.

- Position your models, friends, or family before the photo shoot and ask them to remain in position—this should help when editing photos.

- For outdoor photos, take the photos in quick succession—this will ensure the lighting remains consistent across photos.

- Take as many photos as possible to ensure you have a good variety of shots to choose from for the composition.

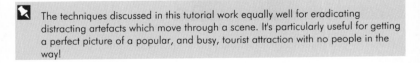

The techniques discussed in this tutorial work equally well for eradicating distracting artefacts which move through a scene. It's particularly useful for getting a perfect picture of a popular, and busy, tourist attraction with no people in the way!

Saving and exporting

 5-15 min

If you've spent a long time correcting your photos in PhotoPlus, or you've created some fantastic graphic art, you'll want to be able to save it and share it with others! This tutorial shows you exactly how to achieve this.

By the end of this tutorial you will be able to:

*   Save your work as a PhotoPlus project file.

*   Create a high quality JPEG (JPG).

*   Export a copy of your work to various photo formats.

*   Resample your work on export to meet various output size requirements.

Let's begin...

Depending on the type of project you've been working on, there are several options open to you when you come to save. You can either save your project as a PhotoPlus project file, save as a copy of the original photo, or export it to a new photo.

 Before you start working on your files, copy the original photos to somewhere safe so you'll always have a set of "digital negatives" or untouched files as a backup.
Saving as a PhotoPlus project file

When you save your work as a PhotoPlus project file, you save the entire project and its settings, such as adjustment layers, masks and paths. If you want to keep the layers editable to make changes later, save your photo as a PhotoPlus project (*.**spp**). You can open, edit and resave a PhotoPlus project file as many times as you want without any loss of quality.

To save your work as a new PhotoPlus project:

1. From the **File** menu, click **Save As**.

2. If you only have a single, **Background** layer and no paths or masks, select PhotoPlus Pictures (*.spp) from the **Save as type** drop-down list, type a name for your file and then click **Save**.
   - or -

   If you've already added any layers, paths or masks, you will see a new dialog asking you to save as a PhotoPlus picture. Click **OK** and then type a name for your file and click **Save**.

Creating a high quality JPEG (JPG)

When you've completely finished editing your photo (be it JPEG or a raw photo processed by the Import Raw dialog), one of the best ways to save your changes is to create an entirely new copy of the photo, i.e. "export" it. This way, you can leave your original file intact. The best format to use in this case is a high quality JPEG.

To export a photo to a high quality JPEG:

1.   From the **File** menu, select **Export**.

2.   In the **Export Optimizer** dialog:

*   Set the **Format** to **JPEG File (JPG)**.

    Note the **Quality** is automatically set to **90%.***

*   Click **Export**.

*When you are working with a photo that has not been edited before, a quality of a JPEG to 90% can result in a file size that is half the size of a JPEG exported at 100%! The loss in photo quality due to compression is undetectable to the human eye.

3. In the **Save As** dialog, type a name for your file and click **Save**.

    Your JPEG photo is saved to the location you specified and ready to print and share!

 If you've been working on an existing photo (raw or JPEG), any Exif information stored within the original photo is automatically added to the exported file.

File size and photo quality

It is possible to reduce the file size of photos (for electronic transfer or placing on websites) by changing the JPEG quality settings. One thing to remember is that as JPEG compression is lossy, i.e., it "throws away data", the photo quickly begins to degrade, especially at lower settings.

You can preview the effect that changing the quality settings (and selecting different file formats) has on your photo and the exported file size in the Export Optimizer dialog. We'll use the following photo to see this in action (zoomed area marked by the red box).

To preview photo export quality:

1. From the **File** menu, select **Export**.

   The **Export Optimizer** dialog opens, displaying your photo along with the estimated exported file size at the current settings.

2. Click ⊕ **Zoom In** to zoom into your photo.

3. Experiment with different types of output file (from the **Format** drop-down list) and **Quality** settings.

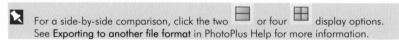

For a side-by-side comparison, click the two ⬒ or four ⊞ display options. See Exporting to another file format in PhotoPlus Help for more information.

You can see the effect that changing the export quality has on the photo. All examples are zoomed in to a ratio of 400%. The original JPEG photo (4272 x 2848 pix) had a file size of 4.32MB.

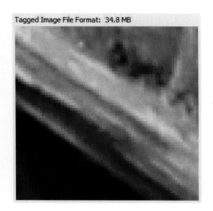
Tagged Image File Format: 34.8 MB

Tagged Image File Format (TIF)

This is the quality experienced using one of the industry standard TIF file types. TIF uses lossless compression and is very good if you still intend on doing some work on the file and don't want to save it as a PhotoPlus project.

It can be used as an intermediate step for raw photos before exporting the final photo as a high quality JPEG. The file size is almost 35MB!

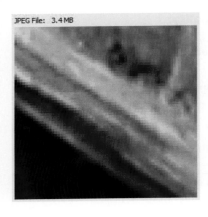

JPEG File (JPG) at 95% quality

This is the quality experienced with a JPEG export set to 95%. As you can see, by comparing it to the photo above, it looks virtually identical (remember, this is at a zoom level of 400%!).

The file size is only 3.4MB. At 100% quality, the file size created is 6.0MB, almost double! (Sometimes a good compromise is a setting of 98%).

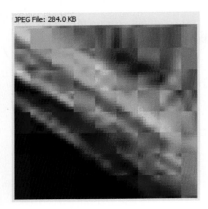

JPEG File (JPG) at 10% quality

This is the quality experienced with a JPEG export set to 10%. The degradation in photo quality is pretty horrendous.

The file size has been reduced to 284KB (0.28MB) but the photo looks very poor.

If you need to display small photos on the web, you would be better resampling them and actually reducing the dimensions of the photo (and as a result, the file size also decreases).

For more information on resampling, see the **Resizing and resampling** tutorial on p. 13.

Resampling a photo on export

Most photos taken straight from the camera have dimensions much bigger than the average monitor display. This means that we can reduce the file size by resizing the photo to fit the screen. Also, as the resolution doesn't need to be as high for a screen photo, it means that we can further reduce file size by exporting the photo as a lower quality JPEG, without affecting the appearance too much. We can do all of this in one step with the **Export Optimizer**. Let's do that now.

Our example photo measures 4272 x 2848 pix and has a file size of 5.93MB. We are going to resample it ready for uploading to our website.

> It is also beneficial to upload a smaller version of your photo to your web page if you are worried about someone "stealing" it. If you resize the photo to 800x600, while it will look okay on screen, it won't be any good for printing.

To resize a photo with the Export Optimizer:

1. From the **File** menu, click **Export**.

    The dialog displays your photo along with the estimated exported file size at the selected quality settings.

    We'll set the size of the photo first.

2. In the **Size** section:

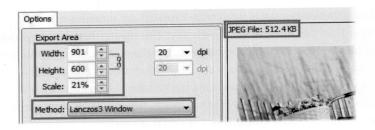

- From the **Method** drop-down list, select **Lanczos 3 Window**.

- Set the **Height** to **600** Pixels and press the **Tab** key. (The **Width** updates automatically.)

  The estimated file size has decreased dramatically. In our example, the file size has gone from 8MB (8000KB) down to around 0.512MB (512KB)!

3. (Optional) If we reduced the JPEG quality setting to 95%, that file size drops to 0.23MB (228KB), yet there's hardly any difference in visual quality!

4. To complete the export, click **Export**, type a name for your file and click **Save**.

Your photo is saved to the chosen folder and is ready to be uploaded to your website or sent via email. (The original remains unchanged.)

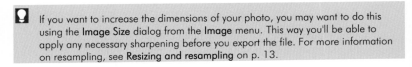

If you want to increase the dimensions of your photo, you may want to do this using the Image Size dialog from the Image menu. This way you'll be able to apply any necessary sharpening before you export the file. For more information on resampling, see Resizing and resampling on p. 13.

Creative Portraits

2

Black and white

15 min

Black and white (greyscale or monochrome) photos can look sophisticated, artistic and modern. They allow you to experiment with contrast and tone without worrying about how colour is affected. In this tutorial, we'll convert a colour photo into a black and white portrait with depth, contrast, and style.

By the end of this tutorial you will be able to:

• Apply and adjust a Channel Mixer adjustment.

• Use a Curves adjustment to increase contrast.

• Use a Curves adjustment to stylize photo with subtle tones.

Let's begin...

- Follow the procedure on p. 24 to open **77.jpg**.

  The photo opens in the workspace.

Convert to black and white with Channel Mixer

The Channel Mixer adjustment can produce one of the best black and white effects, leading to high contrast photos. The best way to start off is to identify which channel has the best contrast, this can be done using the presets on the Channel Mixer adjustment.

To add a Channel Mixer adjustment:

- On the **Adjustments** tab:

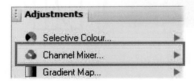

- Click **Channel Mixer**.

  The tab updates to display the settings for the selected adjustment.

- From the **Channel Mixer** drop-down list, select **Monochrome (Green)**.

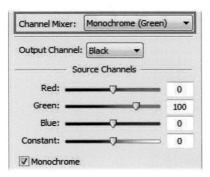

The Output Channel displays Black, the corresponding Source Channels update, and the Monochrome option is selected.

 For portraits, the **Monochrome (Red)** and **Monochrome (Green)** presets generally work best. **Monochrome (Blue)** may be a good option for black and white landscapes.

The photo is converted to black and white.

You can customize the black and white effect by adjusting the Source Channels individually, but we're going to stick with the preset for our photo and use some different adjustments to modify the effect.

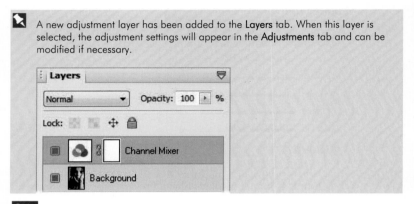

A new adjustment layer has been added to the **Layers** tab. When this layer is selected, the adjustment settings will appear in the **Adjustments** tab and can be modified if necessary.

 Save now! Click **File > Save As** and choose a new name for your file.

Stylizing the black and white effect using Curves

The Curves adjustment lets you manipulate the tonal range of a photo— the spread of lightness values through shadow, midtone, and highlight regions—and control individual colour components. We'll use it first to boost the contrast within the photo and then use it again to add a subtle sultry tone which will enhance the portrait.

To boost contrast:

- On the **Adjustments** tab:

    - Click ⟲ **Back** to return to the list of adjustments.

- Click **Curves**.

  The tab updates to display the settings for the selected adjustment.

- From the **Curves** drop-down list, select **Contrast**.

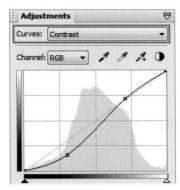

The gentle S-shape deepens the shadows, lightens the highlights, and increases contrast.

The preset makes our photo a little too dark, so we'll tweak the graph's shape to get the desired effect.

- Drag the both points on the graph upwards until it resembles the illustration below.

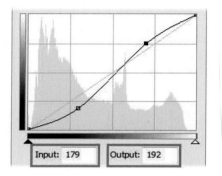

The **Input/Output** values should read around **76/48** for the left point and **179/192** for the right point.

This customized increase in contrast is exactly what we're seeking.

🖫 **Don't forget to save your work!**

We're now going to add a second Curves adjustment, but this time, instead of using it to boost contrast, we're going to use it to introduce some subtle colours to soften the portrait and give it a sultry style and glamour.

To add subtle colour:

- On the **Adjustments** tab:

  - Click 🔙 **Back** to return to the list of adjustments.

  - Click **Curves**.

  - From the **Channel** drop-down list, select **Blue**.

  The tab updates to show the curves for the Blue channel only. We'll add a hint of blue first.

- On the Curves graph, where the gradient intersects the grid at the bottom left, click to create an adjustment point.

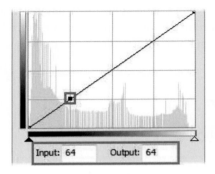

The **Input/Output** values should display at around **64**.

- Drag the point upwards so the **Output** value is set to around **77**.

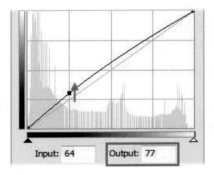

A subtle blue cast has been added to the portrait.

We'll also balance this up with adding a yellow cast.

- On the Curves graph, at the top right part of the gradient, click to create an adjustment point.

- Drag the point downwards until the **Input/Output** values are set to around **192/179**.

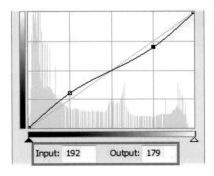

That's it! Our final subtle tone adjustment gives our black and white portrait that touch of added glamour which really makes it stand out.

Why not experiment with the settings throughout this tutorial and apply the effect to your own photos? Don't feel limited to portraits, you can apply the same effect to landscapes as well!

We adjusted the Levels of both of these photos before proceeding with the procedures mentioned in this tutorial. For the landscape photo, we used the Monochrome (Blue) Channel Mixer preset.

Don't forget to save your work! Also see the **Saving and exporting** tutorial on p. 75 for more information.

Colour range

 15 min

In this tutorial, we'll explore a curious, creative use for the **Colour Range** dialog by creating a dramatic portrait. You don't even need to be a creative person to create this effect, all you need is an artistic eye!

By the end of this tutorial you will be able to:

- Extract a photo's shadows and midtones.

- Colour pixels on a layer automatically.

- Add a fill layer to create a new background.

- Group layers together.

- Apply blend modes.

Let's begin...

•   Follow the procedure on p. 24 to open **88.jpg**.

The photo opens in the workspace.

Extracting shadows and midtones

The **Colour Range** dialog allows you to select sampled photo colours as well as specific colours and tones within your photo. We'll use it to select and extract the shadows and midtones from our portrait. We'll then use these tonal areas to get creative with our portrait.

 For more information about selecting using Colour Range, see the **Colour Range** section in **Making a selection** in PhotoPlus Help.

To define shadows:

1.   From the **Select** menu, click **Colour Range**.

2.   In the **Colour Range** dialog, from the **Select** drop-down list, click **Shadows**.

 To preview the selection, select the **Show Selection** option.

3.   Click **OK**.

All the shadows in your photo are selected.

4. From the **Edit** menu, select **Copy**.

5. From the **Layers** menu, select **New Layer from Selection Copy**.

You will now have a new layer dedicated to the shadows in your photo.

6. From the **Select** menu, click **Deselect** (or press **Ctrl+D**).

Now we'll repeat the process to define the midtones in the photo.

 Save now! Click **File > Save As** and choose a new name for your file.

When saving, you may receive a warning message recommending you save your file as a PhotoPlus picture. Click OK to save as an .spp file so you can modify changes at a later date if necessary.

To define midtones:

1. On the **Layers** tab, select the **Background** layer.

2. From the **Select** menu, click **Colour Range**.

3. In the **Colour Range** dialog, from the **Select** drop-down list, click **Midtones** and then click **OK**.

   The midtones in your photo are selected.

4. Press **Ctrl+C** and then press **Ctrl+J**.

   You will now have a two layers, one dedicated to shadows (Layer 1) and another to midtones (Layer 2).

5. From the **Select** menu, click **Deselect** (or press **Ctrl+D**).

Before we continue any further, let's rename our layers to keep our project well organized.

To rename a layer:

1. On the **Layers** tab, double-click **Layer 2**.

2.   In the **Layer Properties** dialog:

  •   In the **Name** input box, rename the layer 'Midtones'.

  •   Click **OK**.

3.   Repeat the above steps to rename **Layer 1** as 'Shadows'.

Now, let's get creative with these shadows and midtones by transforming them into coloured layers.

 Don't forget to save your work!

Filling a layer

We can apply a solid colour fill to our shadow and midtones layers so all pixels in those layers are recoloured while retaining their original transparency values.

To convert a layer to a single colour:

1.   On the **Layers** tab, select the midtones layer.

2.   From the **Edit** menu, click **Fill**.

3. In the **Fill** dialog:

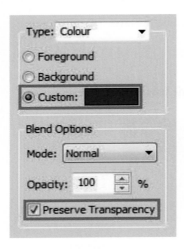

- Select **Custom**.

- Click the **Custom** swatch and in the **Colour Selector** dialog, in the **H**, **S** and **L** input boxes, type '219', '52', and '38', respectively (i.e. HSL=219, 52, 38) then click **OK**.

- Ensure **Preserve Transparency** option is selected.

- Click **OK**.

The midtone layer is converted to blue while retaining each pixel's transparency level.

4. On the **Layers** tab, select the shadows layer and repeat the steps above but define the custom colour as **HSL=219, 52, 23**.

The shadows layer is converted to a darker shade of blue while retaining each pixel's transparency level.

We already have an intriguing portrait and, if you're happy with the design, you can leave it as is. However, let's look at how you can extend the creative possibilities.

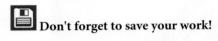 **Don't forget to save your work!**

Adding a new, fill background

We can add a new, fill background to our portrait to create a monochrome photo.

To add a new fill layer:

1. On the **Layers** tab, select the **Background** layer and then click the **New Fill or Adjustment Layer** and select **Fill Layer**.

2. In the **Layer Properties** dialog:

    • In the **Name** input box, type 'Fill'.

    • Click **OK**.

3. In the **Edit Fill** dialog, click the colour swatch.

4. In the **Colour Selector** dialog, in the **H**, **S** and **L** input boxes, type '0', '0', and '100', respectively (i.e. HSL=0, 0, 100).

5. Click **OK** twice to return to the workspace.

6. The new layer is displayed on the Layers tab.

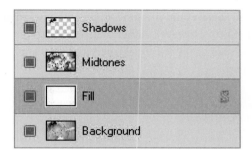

The portrait updates giving it a monochrome design.

Again, this might be the type of design you are seeking for your portrait. However, you can take the portrait in slightly different direction by using blend modes.

 Don't forget to save your work!

Using blend modes

We can blend our coloured shadow and midtone layers with our original photo to give some great effects. However, rather than adjusting their blend modes separately, we can group the tonal layers and then apply the blend mode to the group.

 For more information on blend modes, see **Introduction to blend modes** and **Using blend modes** in PhotoPlus Help.

To group layers:

1. On the **Layers** tab, select the **Midtones** layer and then press the **Ctrl** key and click the **Shadows** layer.

   This selects both layers simultaneously.

   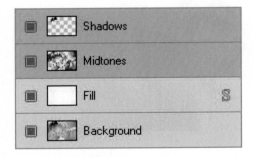

2. Right-click the **Shadows** layer and select **Group Layers**.

Now let's look at getting creative by applying different blend modes to the group.

To apply a blend mode:

* On the **Layers** tab:

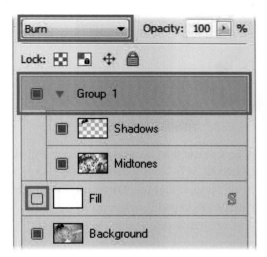

* Click **Hide/Show Layer** to hide the **Fill** layer.

* Click to select **Group 1**.

* From the blend mode drop-down list, select **Burn**.

The monochrome colours within the group blend with the original photo to give a rich portrait.

That's it! Now you know how to use the Colour Range dialog and blend modes to create artistic portraits. Why not try experimenting with other blend modes for a variety of designs? **Lighten**, **Difference**, **Pin Light**, and **Colour** work particularly well at giving dramatically different portraits.

Feel free to experiment with your own photos and apply other colours (you don't have to stick to blue) as you do. You can also adjust the Opacity of Group 1 to give softer blends.

Don't forget to save your work! Also see the **Saving and exporting** tutorial on p. 75 for more information.

Blended texture

 30 min

Blending textures with standard photos can produce artistic and inspiring portraits. We'll walk you through some basic techniques which will allow you to achieve stunning results.

By the end of this tutorial you will be able to:

- Copy photos into a project and reposition layers.

- Blend layers together for dramatic effects.

- Mask a layer to hide and reveal areas of a photo.

- Add an adjustment layer to modify colour.

- Restrict the adjustment so it only affects one layer.

Let's begin...

1. Follow the procedure on p. 24 to open **99.jpg**.

    The photo opens in the workspace.

2. Repeat to open **00.jpg** in the workspace.

We're going to blend our second (texture) photo with our first (portrait) to create a textured portrait.

Copying photos and positioning layers

The first thing we need to do before we can blend these photos together is to ensure they are both in the same project as separate layers.

To copy a photo into a new layer:

1. With **00.jpg** displayed in the workspace, from the **Edit** menu, select **Copy** (or press **Ctrl+C**).

2. On the **Documents** tab, click **99.jpg** to display the portrait in the workspace.

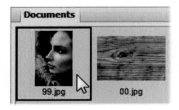

3. From the **Edit** menu, select **Paste** > **As New Layer** (or press **Ctrl+L**).

A new layer, containing the texture, is added to the Layers tab.

The texture displays on top of the portrait.

Our texture is not in the best position to create our blended texture effect. So we need to reposition it before we do anything else.

To reposition content on a layer:

1. On the **Layers** tab, select **Layer 1**.

2. From the **Image** menu, select **Rotate > Layer 90 Anticlockwise**.

3. From the **Image** menu, select **Flip Horizontally > Layer**.

    The texture now has the correct orientation, but it is offset.

4. On the **Tools** toolbar, select the  **Move Tool**.

5. Drag the texture layer left and down until it snaps into place, entirely obscuring the portrait.

Now our texture layer is in position, let's blend it with the portrait layer.

 Don't forget to save your work!

Blending layers

Blending layers together is extremely easy but effective and quickly transforms a portrait. Let's see how it works.

 For more information on blend modes, see **Introduction to blend modes** and **Using blend modes** in PhotoPlus Help.

To apply a blend mode:

- On the **Layers** tab:

- Click to select **Layer 1**.

- From the blend mode drop-down list, select **Multiply**.

The pixels in the texture layer are combined with the pixels in the portrait layer, depending on their lightness values. This immediately gives the portrait a dynamic textured feel.

You may wish to experiment with other blend modes (**Burn, Overlay**, **Vivid Light**, **Difference**, and **Hard Mix** in particular) for equally artistic results, however, we're going to take our portrait onwards using Multiply.

 Don't forget to save your work!

Masking

Currently the texture is applied to all areas of our portrait, regardless of whether they are of our model or the background. We want to limit the texture effect to the model's face and arm only. We can do this using a mask.

 By default, when you click the  Add Layer Mask button, you will apply a Reveal All mask (white mask thumbnail).

To add a mask:

*   On the **Layers** tab:

*   Select **Layer 1**.

*   Click  **Add Layer Mask**.

    A Reveal All mask (indicated by the white mask thumbnail) is added to the texture layer.

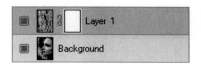

By painting on the mask we can control which layer is visible—those on the texture or portrait.

To edit a mask:

1. On the **Layers** tab, the mask thumbnail should be selected (surrounded by a white outline). If not, click once to select it.

2. On the **Colour** tab, click ■ **Reset Colours** to ensure the foreground swatch is set to black.

   Painting black on a mask will hide the current layer's pixels and make the layer underneath visible.

3. 🖌 On the **Tools** toolbar, from the **Brush Tools** flyout, click the **Paintbrush Tool**.

4. On the **Brush Tip** tab, from the category drop-down list, select **Basic** and then select **Round07** from the gallery (i.e. the **64** pixel soft brush).

5. Carefully start to paint at the top, centre of the portrait by dragging across the photo to remove the texture from between the arm on the left and the face on the right.

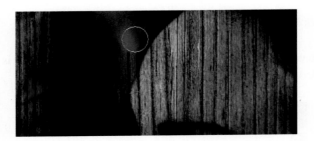

6. Continue painting until your photo resembles the example below.

If you make a mistake along the way, on the **Colour** tab, switch the foreground colour to white and repaint over the mistake.

7. When you are happy, continue painting on other areas of the photo where you wish to remove the texture—i.e. between the model's arm and neck, and between the arm and edge of the photo.

The mask on the Layers tab will update to show a representation of the areas you have painted.

The texture in our portrait is now confined to our model, giving the illusion she has been carved out of wood.

To add further intrigue to our blended texture portrait, we also removed the texture from the model's eye.

You may wish to leave your portrait as it is, but we'll walk you through adjusting the colour of the textured layer to help enhance the portrait.

Adding texture colour

The original texture is a rather dull grey tone which gives our portrait a mysterious but somewhat dark feel. We can adjust the colour of the texture using an adjustment layer.

To colourize a layer:

1. On the **Layers** tab, select **Layer 1**.

2. On the **Adjustments** tab:

    -   Click **Colourize**.

        The tab updates to display the settings for the selected adjustment.

- Type in the input boxes to set the **Hue**, **Saturation**, and **Lightness** to **38**, **36**, and **0**, respectively.

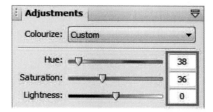

Our photo instantly updates to give a monochrome **portrait design**.

This monochrome **design may** be exactly what **you want for** the portrait. However, **the** adjustment has **eradicated the** colour along **the model's arms.** These colours **can be recovered** by restricting **the adjustment to** the texture layer **below only.**

To restrict the scope of an adjustment:

- On the **Layers** tab, right-click the **Colourize** layer and select **Clip to Layer Below**.

The Colourize layer becomes indented and a double-headed arrow indicates the adjustment is restricted to the texture layer.

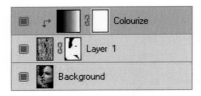

The portrait updates, displaying the original colours in a bold and dramatic way.

That's it! The blended texture portrait is now complete. Why not experiment with your own photos using the texture provided or other textures which you might have available?

 For more information on clipping to layers, see **Using adjustment layers: Clipping adjustment layers** in PhotoPlus Help.

Don't forget to save your work! Also see the **Saving and exporting** tutorial on p. 75 for more information.

Creative
Showcase

3

Brushes

PhotoPlus provides a large collection of brush tips to help you get creative and use with your photos.

To select a brush tip:

1. On the **Tools** toolbar, from the **Brush Tools** flyout, select **Paintbrush Tool**.

2. On the **Brush Tip** tab, from the category drop-down list, select a category.

    The category's gallery is displayed in the tab. Each gallery shows the brush tip and stroke.

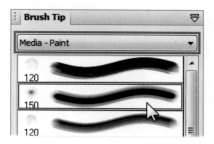

3. Click to select a preset brush tip from the gallery and then drag across your photo to paint your lines.

We'll showcase the **Media - Paint**, **Effects - Clouds**, and **Effects - Grunged** sub-categories next.

Media - Paint

Effects - Clouds

Effects - Grunged

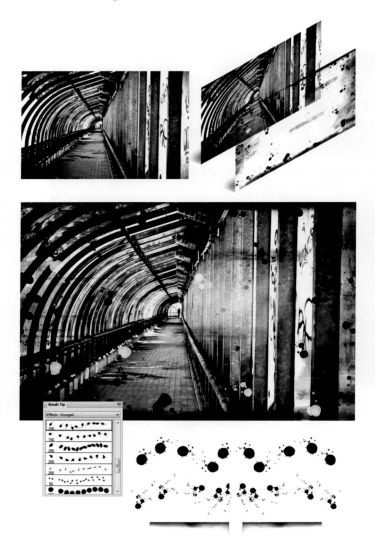

Samples

PhotoPlus installs with sample files which show how the program can be used to modify photos or create stunning digital art. These sample files are available directly from the **Startup Assistant**.

To open a PhotoPlus sample file:

1. On the **File** menu, click **Startup Assistant**.

2. On the left, click **Open**.

3. Click **Sample Files**.

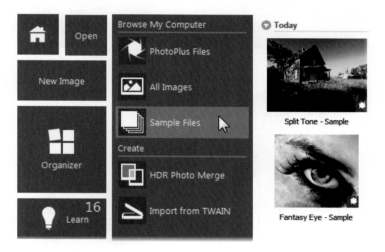

4. In the **Open** dialog, select your sample file, and then click **Open**.

We'll showcase the **Split Tone**, **Fantasy Eye**, and **Photo Restoration** samples next.

Split Tone

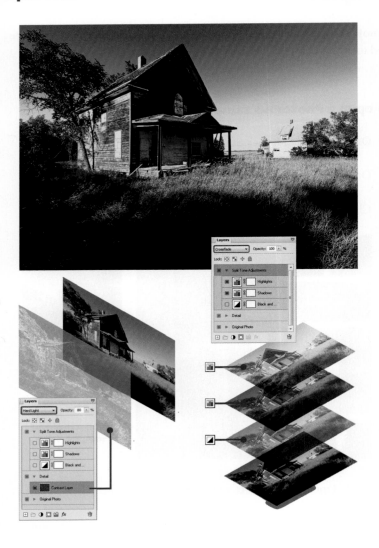

Fantasy Eye

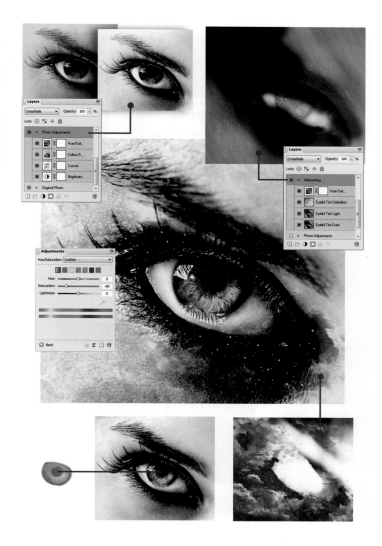

Photo Restoration

Filter Gallery

The Filter Gallery offers an environment for applying single or multiple filter effects. The expandable categories have a thumbnail gallery displaying the range of effects available.

To add a Filter Gallery effect:

1. On the **Photo Studio** toolbar, click **Filter Gallery**.

    The **Filter Gallery** dialog will launch displaying a preview of your photo and the **Artistic** category open by default.

2. Click to open a category on the right, and click a gallery thumbnail to apply the effect to your photo.

For more information about the Filter Gallery, see Using the Filter Gallery in PhotoPlus Help.

We'll showcase the **Artistic**, **Stylistic**, and more effects next.

Artistic

Stylistic

More...

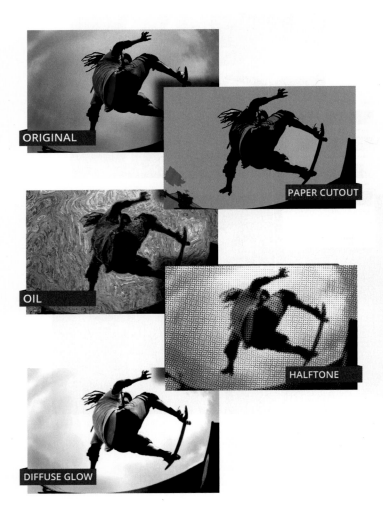